Book

IN RECITAL®
with Jazz, Blues, & Rags

ABOUT THE SERIES • A NOTE TO THE TEACHER

In Recital® with Jazz, Blues, & Rags is a series that focuses on wonderful jazz, blues, and ragtime pieces, guaranteed to motivate your students! The fine composers and arrangers of this series have created engaging originals and arrangements which have been carefully leveled to ensure success with this repertoire. We know that in order to motivate, the teacher must challenge the student with attainable goals. This series makes that possible while also providing a perfect way for students to learn about jazz, blues, and rags! This series complements other FJH publications and can be used alongside any method. Students will find even more joy in these jazz, blues, and rags when they read the "About the Pieces and Composers" section in the front and back of the books. The books include CDs with complete performances to assist with recital preparation.

 Use the enclosed CD as a teaching and motivational tool. Have your students listen to the recordings and discuss interpretation and style with you!

Production: Frank J. Hackinson
Production Coordinators: Joyce Loke and Philip Groeber
Art Direction: Terpstra Design, San Francisco, CA
Cover and Interior Art Concepts: Helen Marlais
Cover and Interior Illustrations: Sophie Library
Engraving: Tempo Music Press, Inc.
Printer: Tempo Music Press, Inc.

ISBN-13: 978-1-56939-690-2

Copyright © 2008 by THE FJH MUSIC COMPANY INC. (ASCAP).
2525 Davie Road, Suite 360, Fort Lauderdale, Florida 33317-7424
International Copyright Secured. All Rights Reserved. Printed in U.S.A.

WARNING! The music, text, design, and graphics in this publication, unless otherwise indicated, are copyrighted by The FJH Music Company Inc. and are protected by copyright law. Any duplication is an infringement of U.S. copyright law.

ORGANIZATION OF THE SERIES
IN RECITAL® WITH JAZZ, BLUES, & RAGS

The series is carefully leveled into the following six categories: Early Elementary, Elementary, Late Elementary, Early Intermediate, Intermediate, and Late Intermediate. Each of the works has been selected for its artistic as well as its pedagogical merit.

Book Three — Late Elementary, reinforces the following concepts:

- Eighth notes and eighth note rests.

- Students learn to play with a swing beat and with syncopation.

- Students reinforce their comprehension of tonic and dominant notes and basic chord progressions.

- Five-finger patterns as well as patterns that extend from a five-finger pattern are used.

- Blocked and broken chords and intervals.

- Musical details employed are the following: *crescendo, diminuendo, ritardando, glissando, D.S. al Coda, subito.*

- Students play in a variety of different keys (using key signatures).

- Students play with many different articulations.

Students can be encouraged to practice the pieces marked "swing" with straight eighth notes first, and then when the rhythm is secure, the eighth notes can be "swung."

Most of the pieces in Book Three may be played as solos. Two of the solos have teacher duet parts to enhance the overall sound of the piece. *Echoes from the Snowball Club* and *Summer Rain* were composed as equal-part duets.

TABLE OF CONTENTS

ABOUT THE PIECES AND COMPOSERS

Grey's Blues, by David Karp

This jazzy and fun original solo was inspired by the birth of David Karp's grandson Grey in the spring of 2007. The blues was a big inspiration for jazz and both kinds of music use similar chords and rhythms to make "riffs," even though the sounds are different. The blues generally has a more laid back, relaxed feel, whereas jazz can be more upbeat. Regardless of the title, as you play, decide for yourself whether this piece is more bluesy or jazzy!

Frankie and Johnny, Traditional

This traditional American song has a number of versions created by various musicians, but the original is said to date back as early as the 1850s. It is also believed to have been sung at the Siege of Vicksburg, significant battle of the American Civil War.

This folk song has become so popular that nearly 256 recordings have been made by various musicians such as Lead Belly, Stevie Wonder, Bob Dylan, and Johnny Cash to name a few. In addition, it has been recorded by famous jazz performers such as Duke Ellington, Louis Armstrong, and Benny Goodman. The story conveyed by the lyrics has been the basis for a number of movies with the same or similar titles.

Alarm Clock Blues, by Jimmy Steiger and Neuman Fier

This charming piece of music was written in 1921 as a novelty song. These songs are usually written in a humorous vein and talk about everyday events.

Alarm Clock Blues is about a person trying to enjoy a "peaceful snooze" but is awoken every morning by his alarm clock. His advice, which is quite obvious, is to turn off your alarm clock if you do not want your sleep to be disturbed.

Wade in the Water, by Ramsey Lewis

Wade in the Water is a traditional African-American spiritual which was popularized by Ramsey Lewis, who added his own touch to it.

Ramsey Lewis is an American pianist from Chicago who started studying the piano at the age of four. When he was fifteen he joined a quartet led by the saxophonist Wallace Burton. By the time he was twenty years old, he took over leadership of the band, now a trio, which became very successful. Their album *The In Crowd* sold over a million copies and went on to win the Grammy for best jazz recording by a small group. Lewis still maintains an active performance schedule all over the United States.

Echoes from the Snowball Club, by Harry P. Guy

Harry Guy was born in 1870 in Ohio but moved to various cities to pursue higher studies in music and later, his career. When he was around eight years old, he began studying the piano, the pipe organ, and the violin. Despite being a very talented composer and arranger, his extreme modesty kept him from achieving the wealth and fame he could have earned.

This piece was Harry Guy's first ragtime waltz (a rag written in $\frac{3}{4}$ time) and also his most popular composition.

Peacherine Rag, by Scott Joplin

Scott Joplin is one of the most popular ragtime composers of all time. Although he wrote other forms of music, he is predominantly known for his piano rags. He and his long-time publisher, John Stark, referred to his music as "classic rags," comparing their quality to that of the European classics. Joplin always attempted to preserve the quality of his works by pleading that performers of his music strive to play his rags with just as much skill and care as he showed in composing them.

He was awarded the Pulitzer Prize in 1976, fifty-nine years after his death, and a commemorative postage stamp was released in his honor in 1983.

Zigzag, by Lee Evans

To zigzag means to move by sharp turns in alternating directions, just as this swing jazz composition begins. The energetic sound of the swing jazz style requires a lot of keyboard range in order to create a big band swing dance feel. This original composition uses the idea of melodic intervals of seconds and traditional jazz syncopations to make your hands feel as though they are dancing up and down the keyboard.

The Entertainer, by Scott Joplin

Scott Joplin moved to various cities during the course of his career. In 1901 he moved to St. Louis, Missouri, and spent most of his time composing and teaching, putting performing on the back burner. He wrote *The Entertainer* in 1902, which, with a few other rags such as *The Easy Winners* and *The Strenuous Life,* increased his popularity.

As a child, Joplin did not have much access to education. However, his mother took a very active interest and ensured that he received good training at the hands of the German musician, Julius Weiss.

for Grey Geller Golman

Grey's Blues

David Karp

Swing it! (♩ = ca. 132) (♫ = ♩³♪)

To Coda ⊕

mf

Copyright © 2008 The FJH Music Company Inc. (ASCAP).
International Copyright Secured.   Made in U.S.A.   All Rights Reserved.

Frankie and Johnny

Traditional   arr. Kevin Costley

With a moderate swing (♩ = ca. 112)

This arrangement © 2008 The FJH Music Company Inc. (ASCAP).
International Copyright Secured.   Made in U.S.A.   All Rights Reserved.

8   FJH

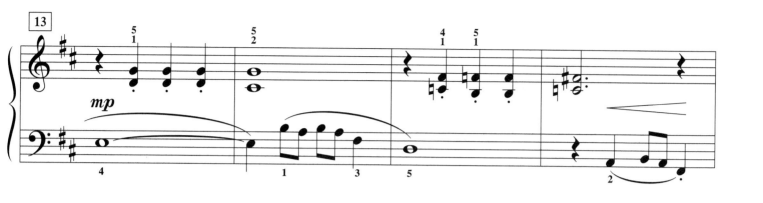

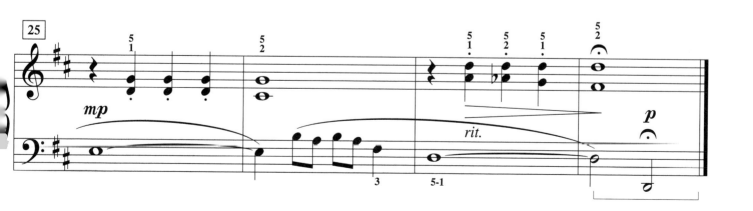

741

Alarm Clock Blues

Jimmy Steiger and Neuman Fier   arr. Edwin McLean

With a honky-tonk swing (♩ = ca. 132) (♫ = ♩³♪)

mf

mp

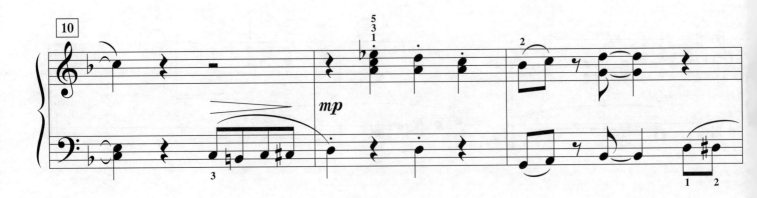

This arrangement © 2008 Frank J. Hackinson Publishing Company (BMI).
International Copyright Secured.   Made in U.S.A.   All Rights Reserved.

FJH

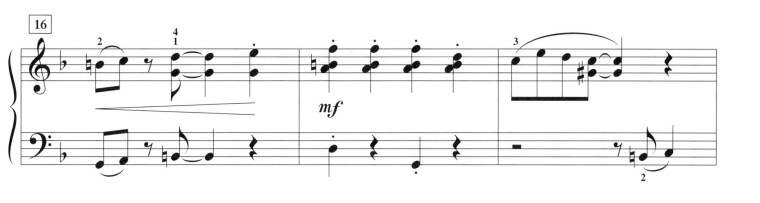

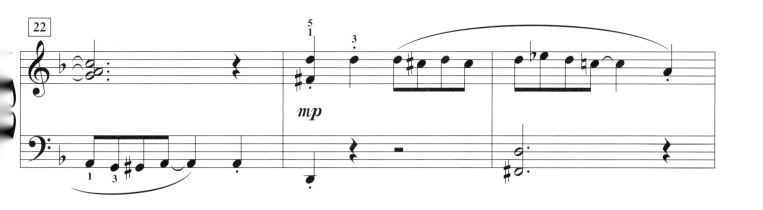

741

Wade in the Water

Ramsey Lewis   arr. Robert Schultz

Moderately fast; even ♫ (♩ = ca. 138)

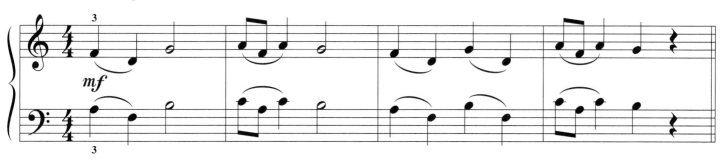

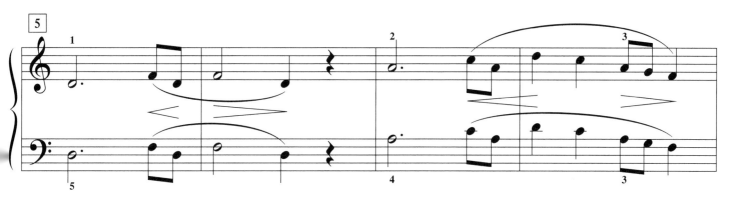

Teacher Duet: (*Student plays one octave higher*)

Suggested introduction: Play measures 1-2 twice. Then, start from the beginning with the student.

Copyright © 1966 (Renewed) by Embassy Music Corporation (BMI).
This arrangement © 2008 Embassy Music Corporation (BMI). Reprinted by Permission.
International Copyright Secured.   Made in U.S.A.   All Rights Reserved.

FJH

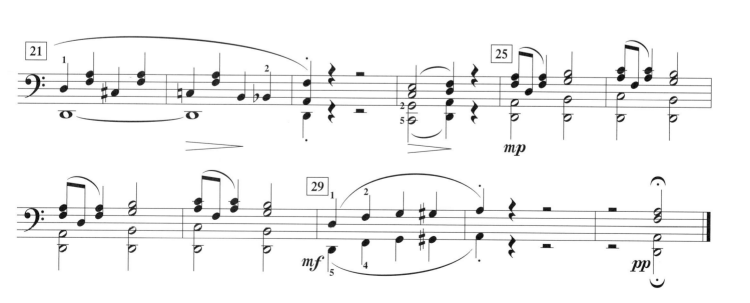

Echoes from the Snowball Club

Harry P. Guy   arr. Jason Sifford

Secondo

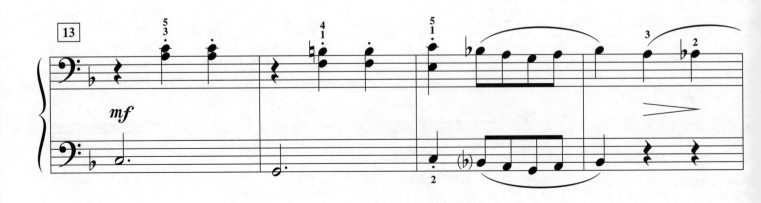

This arrangement © 2008 The FJH Music Company Inc. (ASCAP).
International Copyright Secured.   Made in U.S.A.   All Rights Reserved.

FJH

Echoes from the Snowball Club

Harry P. Guy   arr. Jason Sifford

Primo

Waltz tempo (♩ = ca. 120)

Play both hands one octave higher throughout

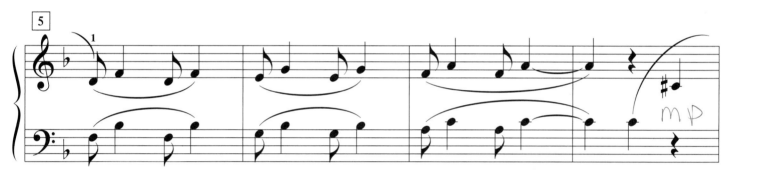

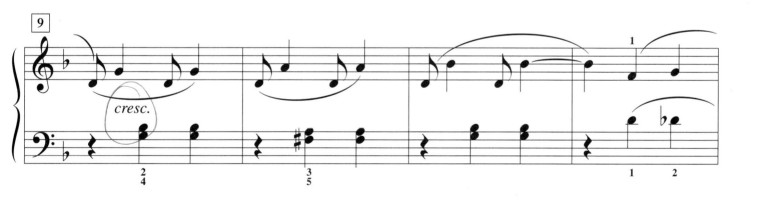

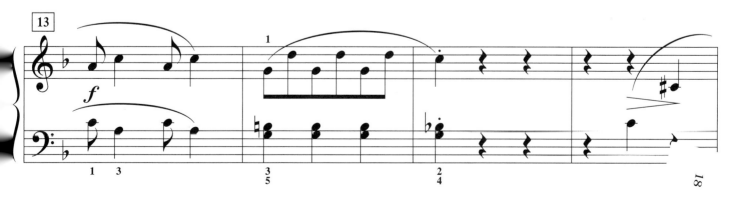

This arrangement © 2008 The FJH Music Company Inc. (ASCAP).
International Copyright Secured.   Made in U.S.A.   All Rights Reserved.

Secondo

Primo

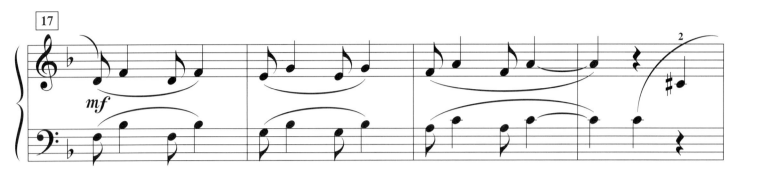

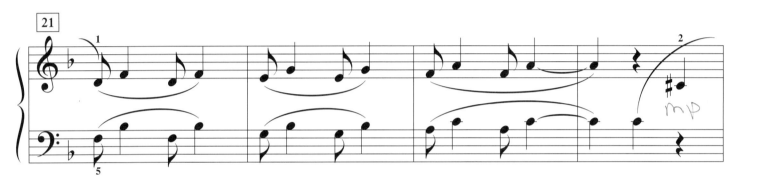

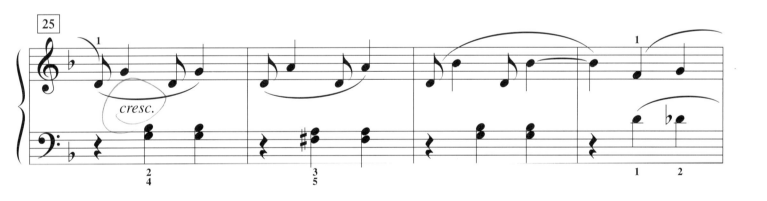

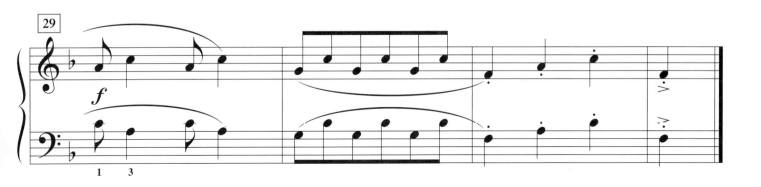

Peacherine Rag

Scott Joplin   arr. Timothy Brown

This arrangement © 2008 The FJH Music Company Inc. (ASCAP).
International Copyright Secured.   Made in U.S.A.   All Rights Reserved.

FJH1

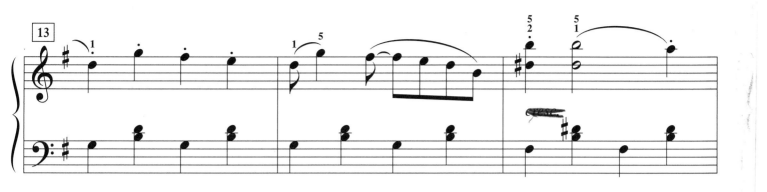

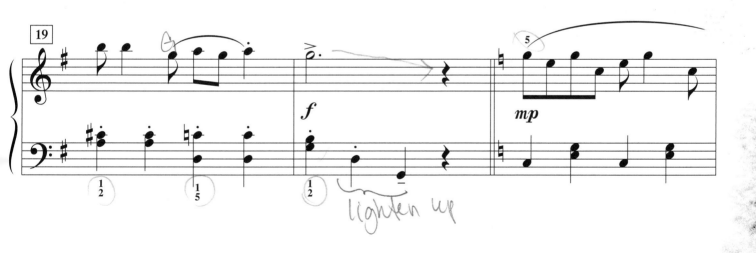

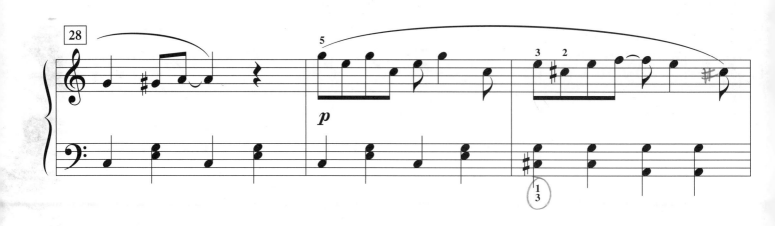

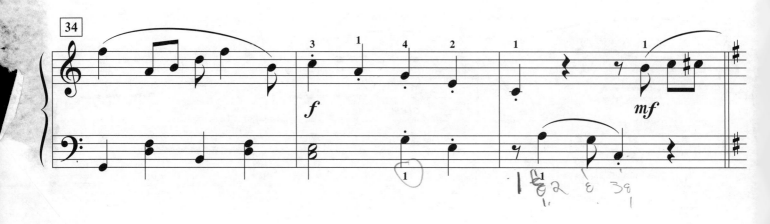

FJH

Zigzag

Lee Evans

With a light swing (♩ = ca. 160) (♫ = ♩♪³)

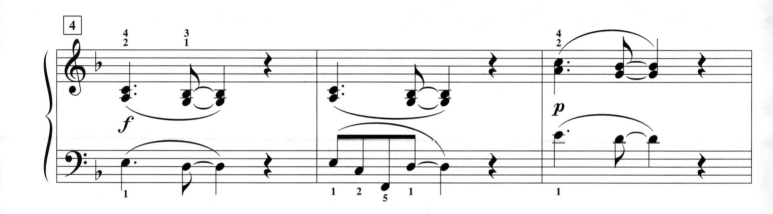

Copyright © 2008 The FJH Music Company Inc. (ASCAP).
International Copyright Secured.   Made in U.S.A.   All Rights Reserved.

FJH

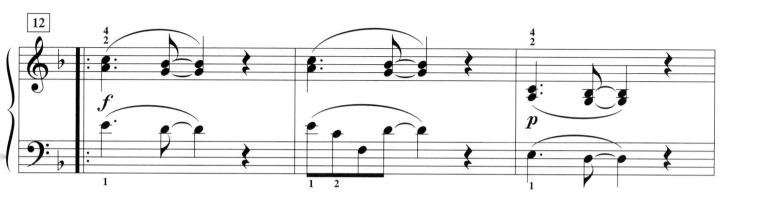

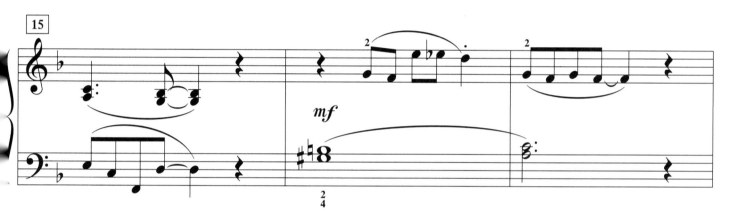

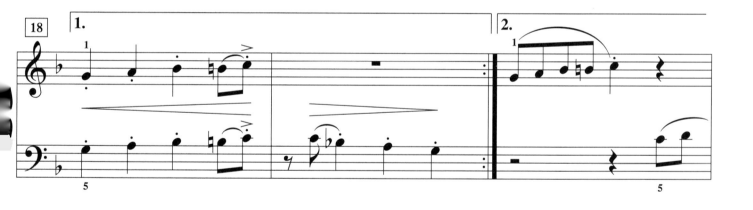

The Entertainer

Scott Joplin   arr. Kevin Olson

Not fast (♩ = ca. 138)

This arrangement © 2008 The FJH Music Company Inc. (ASCAP).
International Copyright Secured.   Made in U.S.A.   All Rights Reserved.

FJI

D.S. 𝄋 al Coda

Coda

Take Me Out to the Ball Game

Music: Albert von Tilzer   Lyrics: Jack Norworth   arr. Edwin McLean

With a happy swing (♩ = ca. 132-144) (♫ = ♩³♪)

Take me out to the

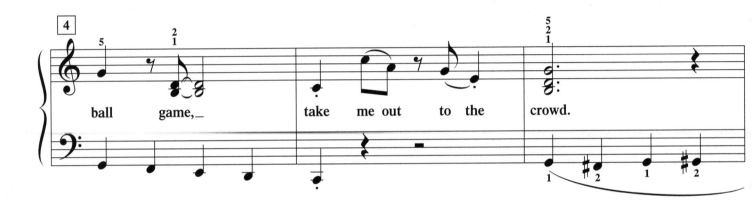

ball game,— take me out to the crowd.

Buy me some pea - nuts and Crack - er Jack;— I don't_ care if I

nev - er get back. And_ it's root, root, root for the home team,_ if_

This arrangement © 2008 Frank J. Hackinson Publishing Company (BMI).
International Copyright Secured.   Made in U.S.A.   All Rights Reserved.

FJ

they   don't win___ it's   a   shame.   For it's   one,   two,

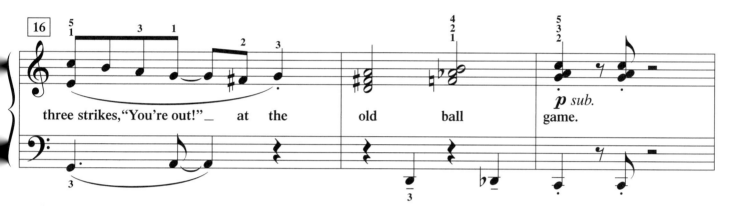

three strikes, "You're out!" __   at   the   old   ball   game.

Ain't We Got Fun

Richard A. Whiting, Raymond Egan, and Gus Kahn
arr. Robert Schultz

Relaxed

Moderately; even ♪'s (♩ = 72)

espressivo

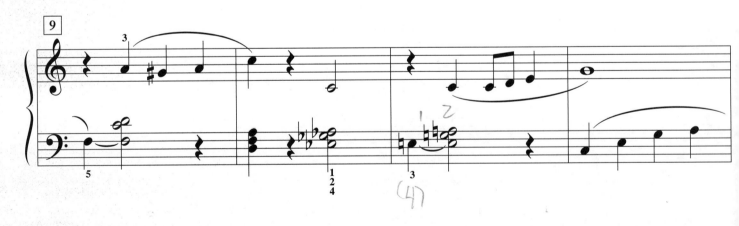

This arrangement © 2008 The FJH Music Company Inc. (ASCAP).
International Copyright Secured.   Made in U.S.A.   All Rights Reserved.

Mama Don't 'Low

Traditional   arr. Edwin McLean

With a medium swing (♩ = 132) (♪♪ = ♪³♪)

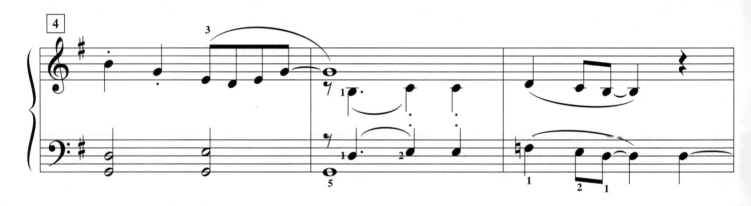

This arrangement © 2008 Frank J. Hackinson Publishing Company (BMI).
International Copyright Secured.   Made in U.S.A.   All Rights Reserved.

FJH

Summer Rain

Edwin McLean

Secondo

Moderately; lyrically (♩ = 104) (no swing)
Play both hands as written

Copyright © 2008 Frank J. Hackinson Publishing Company (BMI).
International Copyright Secured.   Made in U.S.A.   All Rights Reserved.

FJI

Summer Rain

Edwin McLean

Primo

Moderately; lyrically (♩ = 104) (no swing)

Play both hands one octave higher throughout

Copyright © 2008 Frank J. Hackinson Publishing Company (BMI).
International Copyright Secured.   Made in U.S.A.   All Rights Reserved.

Secondo

Primo

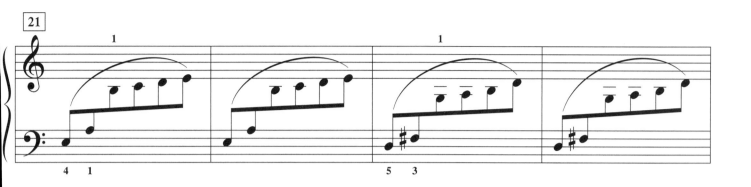

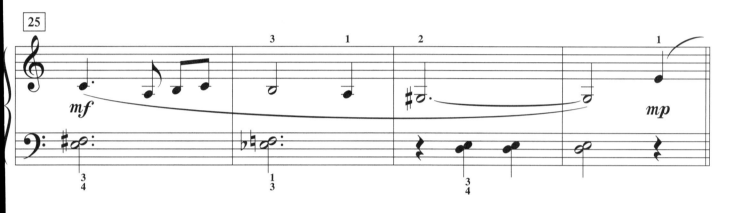

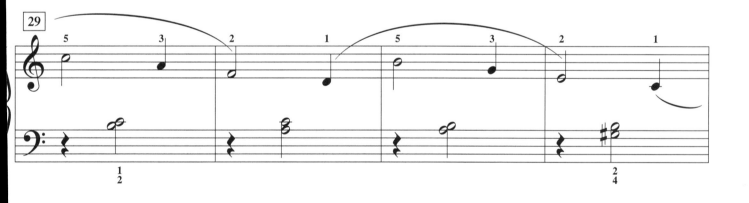

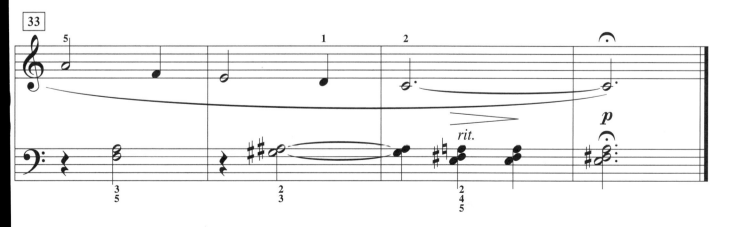

Crazy Blues

Perry Bradford   arr. Kevin Olson

With a lazy swing (♩ = ca. 120)

Teacher Duet: (*Student plays as written*)

This arrangement © 2008 The FJH Music Company Inc. (ASCAP).
International Copyright Secured.   Made in U.S.A.   All Rights Reserved.

ABOUT THE PIECES AND COMPOSERS

Take Me Out to the Ball Game, by Albert von Tilzer and Jack Norworth

This song has become the unofficial anthem of baseball and is traditionally sung during the seventh inning.

Jack Norworth, who wrote the lyrics in 1908, is said to have been inspired by a sign that read "Baseball Today - Polo Grounds" which he saw while riding a subway train. Albert von Tilzer set these lyrics to music in the same year. It is interesting to note that neither von Tilzer nor Norworth had ever seen a baseball game prior to writing this song. In fact, the first game they ever watched was decades after they wrote this favorite.

Ain't We Got Fun, by Richard A. Whiting, Raymond Egan, and Gus Kahn

Richard Whiting was an American composer who taught himself the piano and music theory. When he started composing he convinced his father to publish his first few pieces. He wrote *Ain't We Got Fun* in 1921 after he moved to New York. Raymond Egan was originally from Canada but his family moved to the U.S. when he was only two years old. Gus Kahn was born in Germany but immigrated with his family to the U.S. in 1890 when he was four years old.

All three writers of this song were inducted into The Songwriters Hall of Fame in 1970 for their contribution to music.

This standard talks about a happy couple who stay very positive in their outlook on life despite the fact that their bills are unpaid, there are collectors at the door, and the stork just brought them twin babies. It has been recorded by many artists and has also been quoted in the novel *The Great Gatsby* by F. Scott Fitzgerald.

Mama Don't 'Low, Traditional

This traditional song talks about a child disobeying his mother. Despite his mother not permitting him to play the banjo or guitar, or to talk or sing, the child decides to do so anyway. There is no definite interpretation of the lyrics, but one can infer that it is about a child rebelling against his strict mother.

Banjos and guitars were commonly used by Dixieland bands—ensembles which played Dixieland music, which is a style of jazz. This arrangement of *Mama Don't 'Low* has a bluesy, gospel feel.

Summer Rain, by Edwin McLean

Summer Rain is a soft and gentle ballad, like the refreshing rains of summer that are so welcome after days of dry heat. The piece features long, lyrical, and melodic phrases that keep the pace even and flowing. There is a brief melody in a major key in the B section, after which the piece closes with a return to the melody in a minor key. This relaxing piece is a breath of fresh, calm air in a collection of bustling and bouncy rags and jazz!

Crazy Blues, by Perry Bradford

Perry Bradford was a music director, composer, and pianist. He was also known by his nickname, Mule, which he is believed to have acquired after being featured the vaudeville song, *Whoa, Mule*.

He wrote the song *Harlem Blues* in 1918 for a musical revue titled *Made in Harlem*. A musical revue is a satirical stage production which frequently uses contemporary figures, news, or literature as its subject.

In 1920, he re-titled *Harlem Blues* as *Crazy Blues* and Mamie Smith recorded it at her second recording session that same year. *Crazy Blues* went on to sell more than a million copies and started the trend towards blues singing.

ABOUT THE ARRANGERS

Timothy Brown

Timothy Brown did his undergraduate studies at Bowling Green State University and received his master's degree in piano performance from the University of North Texas. His past teachers include Adam Wodnicki, Newel Kay Brown and Robert Xavier Rodriguez. He was a recipient of a research fellowship from Royal Holloway, University of London, where he performed his postgraduate studies in music composition and orchestration with the English composer, Brian Lock. He later continued his research at the well known Accademia Nazionale di Santa Cecilia in Rome, Italy.

His numerous credits as a composer include the first prize at the Aliénor International Harpsichord Competition for his harpsichord solo *Suite Española* (Centaur records). His recent programs include his original compositions showcased at the Spoleto Music Festival, and the Library of Congress Concert Series in Washington D.C. His recent commissions and performances include world premieres by the Chapman University Chamber Orchestra and Concert Choir, the Carter Albrecht Music Foundation, the Rodgers Center for Holocaust Education, and the Daniel Pearl Music Foundation. Timothy Brown is an exclusive composer/clinician for The FJH Music Company Inc. (ASCAP)

Kevin Costley

Kevin Costley holds several graduate degrees in the areas of elementary education and piano pedagogy, and literature, including a doctorate from Kansas State University. For nearly two decades, he was owner and director of The Keyboard Academy, specializing in innovative small group instruction. Kevin served for several years as head of the music department and on the keyboard faculty of Messenger College in Joplin, Missouri.

Kevin is a standing faculty member of Inspiration Point Fine Arts Colony piano and string camp, where he performs and teaches private piano, ensemble classes, and composition. He conducts child development seminars, writes for national publications, serves as a clinician for piano workshops, and adjudicates numerous piano festivals and competitions. Presently, Dr. Costley is an associate professor of early childhood education at Arkansas Tech University in Russellville, Arkansas.

Lee Evans

Lee Evans, professor of music and former chairperson of the Theatre & Fine Arts Department of Pace University in New York City, graduated from New York City's High School of Music & Art and completed degrees at New York University and Columbia University, receiving his Master of Arts and Doctor of Education from the latter. In addition to college level teaching, he also taught briefly at the junior and high school levels. Professionally, he concertized for ten consecutive seasons under the auspices of Columbia Artists Management, and has performed on some of the world's most prestigious stages, including the White House. He has been music coordinator/director for Tom Jones, Engelbert Humperdinck, Carol Channing, Cat Stevens, and Emerson, Lake, & Palmer. He is an acclaimed educator, performer, lecturer, composer, and arranger, and is author of over 90 published music books. Dr. Evans has worked to show it is possible for classical piano teachers with no prior jazz experience to teach jazz concepts with the same skill and discipline as classical music. Dr. Evans has succeeded in bringing an understanding of and feeling for jazz to keyboard students and teachers.

David Karp

David Karp—nationally known pianist, composer, educator, lecturer, and author—holds degrees from Manhattan School of Music and the University of Colorado. Dr. Karp is professor of music and director of the National Piano Teachers Institute at SMU's Meadows School of the Arts, where he teaches courses in piano performance, composition, theory and aural skills, improvisation, and class piano techniques for the college teacher. Former students are now professionally engaged on college campuses throughout the United States. Dr. Karp has performed, lectured, and conducted workshops and seminars at many colleges and universities from Alaska to New Hampshire, and as far away as Taiwan.

In 1993, Dr. Karp was honored with the establishment of the David Karp Piano Festival, an annual event held at Kilgore College in Kilgore, Texas, in which over 200 students perform and are judged on Karp compositions. Dr. Karp enjoys playing tennis, reading books, and watching movies. During the summer, he spends time practicing and composing at his cottage in Maine. Dr. and Mrs. Karp have three married children and seven grandchildren.

Edwin McLean

Edwin McLean is a composer living in Chapel Hill, North Carolina. He is a graduate of the Yale School of Music, where he studied with Krzysztof Penderecki and Jacob Druckman. He also holds a master's degree in music theory and a bachelor's degree in piano performance from the University of Colorado. Mr. McLean has authored over 200 publications for The FJH Music Company, ranging from *The FJH Classic Music Dictionary* to original works for pianists from beginner to advanced. His highly-acclaimed works for harpsichord have been performed internationally and are available on the Miami Bach Society recording, *Edwin McLean: Sonatas for 1, 2, and 3 Harpsichords*. His 2011 solo jazz piano album *Don't Say Goodbye* (CD1043) includes many of his advanced works for piano published by FJH.

Edwin McLean began his career as a professional arranger. Currently, he is senior editor for The FJH Music Company Inc.

Kevin Olson

Kevin Olson is an active pianist, composer, and member of the piano faculty at Utah State University, where he teaches piano literature, pedagogy, and accompanying courses. In addition to his collegiate teaching responsibilities, Kevin directs the Utah State Youth Conservatory, which provides weekly group and private piano instruction to more than 200 pre-college community students. The National Association of Schools of Music has recently recognized the Conservatory as a model for pre-college piano instruction programs. Before teaching at Utah State, he was on the faculty at Elmhurst College near Chicago and Humboldt State University in northern California. A native of Utah, Kevin began composing at age five. When he was twelve, his composition, *An American Trainride*, received the Overall First Prize at the 1983 National PTA Convention at Albuquerque, New Mexico. Since then he has been a Composer in Residence at the National Conference on Piano Pedagogy, and has written music commissioned and performed by groups such as the American Piano Quartet, Chicago a cappella, the Rich Matteson Jazz Festival, and several piano teacher associations around the country.

Kevin maintains a large piano studio, teaching students of a variety of ages and abilities. Many of the needs of his own piano students have inspired more than 100 books and solos published by The FJH Music Company Inc., which he joined as a writer in 1994.

Robert Schultz

Robert Schultz, composer, arranger, and editor, has achieved international fame during his career in the music publishing industry. The Schultz Piano Library, established in 1980, has included more than 500 publications of classical works, popular arrangements, and Schultz's original compositions in editions for pianists of every level from the beginner through the concert artist. In addition to his extensive library of published piano works, Schultz's output includes original orchestral works, chamber music, works for solo instruments, and vocal music.

Schultz has presented his published editions at workshops, clinics, and convention showcases throughout the United States and Canada. He is a long-standing member of ASCAP and has served as president of the Miami Music Teachers Association. Mr. Schultz's original piano compositions and transcriptions are featured on the compact disc recordings *Visions of Dunbar* and *Tina Faigen Plays Piano Transcriptions*, released on the ACA Digital label and available worldwide. His published original works for concert artists are noted in Maurice Hinson's *Guide to the Pianist's Repertoire, Third Edition*. He currently devotes his full time to composing and arranging. In-depth information about Robert Schultz and The Schultz Piano Library is available at the Website www.schultzmusic.com.

Jason Sifford

Dr. Jason Sifford is a versatile pianist with a wide range of interests. As a performer, his repertoire covers the entire pianistic spectrum. He particularly enjoys the music of Haydn, Schumann, Brahms, and Albéniz, and feels equally at home on the concert stage, in a pit orchestra, or in a late-night jazz club, comfortable with both classical and jazz styles. Dr. Sifford is also an active pedagogue, lecturing on such diverse topics as performance practice, jazz ensemble playing, technical development in young pianists, and the use of technology in the studio.

Dr. Sifford holds degrees in piano performance from Southwest Missouri State University and Louisiana State University, and has a doctorate in piano performance and pedagogy from the University of Michigan. He has studied piano with Logan Skelton, Constance Carroll, and Arthur Greene, and pedagogy with Joanne Smith and Donald Morelock. Most recently, Dr. Sifford served on the faculty of Texas Tech University and as principal pianist and teaching artist for the Lubbock Symphony Orchestra. He is currently a freelance pianist, composer, and teacher residing in El Paso, Texas, with his wife, Renée.

USING THE CD

A great way to prepare these jazz, blues, and rag pieces is to use the CD.

Listen to the complete performances of all the pieces. In this way, you will understand the different style and character of each piece. Enjoy listening to these pieces anywhere, anytime! Listen to them casually (as background music) or attentively. After you have listened to the CD, you might discuss interpretation with your teacher and follow along with your score as you listen.

About the duets: The duets have *primo* and *secondo* parts. (These Italian music terms are pronounced "PREE-moh" and "seh-KOHN-doh.")

Remember that the *primo* part is always on the right-hand side of the book, while the *secondo* part is always on the left-hand side of the book. The *primo* part plays on the upper half of the piano; the *secondo* part plays on the lower half.